INTR

I looked deeply into Diane's eyes. "Three weeks ago, I was diagnosed with pancreatic cancer," she said. "It has spread to my liver and spleen." I held her hand as we talked about her life and what mattered most—her husband, children, grandchildren, and her relationship with God. She said, "I have to make room for life and give today a chance."

Her words echo over and over in my mind. Many of us have lives that are busy and hectic—lots of motion and repetition with very little meaning. We're constantly on our way to the next place, seldom taking a moment to soak in life.

As with Diane, we will all have days when we're neck-deep in tough times: friends who forget us, spouses who complain, pressures that surface, creditors calling, and then, those awful days when the cemetery dirt is still fresh.

To bring meaning, happiness, and purpose back into our lives, we must let go of our attachment to other people's opinions, our learned behaviors, our self-doubts, and our poor self-images. These keep us from living the rich, meaningful, and exciting lives that we truly deserve.

Lent is a prime time to make room for life and give every day a chance. Again, like Diane, when we prepare to leave this world, we want to be at peace and know that we've made a difference. I offer the following practical and motivating reflections to help you realign your priorities and uncover a real and understandable approach to daily living.

I offer suggestions about "how to" and "what to" pursue, so that you can bring the results into your life and finally set free the person you are deep inside. My hope is that you will also discover a new spring to your step, recognize your magnificence, and find new meaning in your relationship with God.

February 22 | Ash Wednesday

JOEL 2:12–18 • 2 CORINTHIANS 5:20—6:2 • MATTHEW 6:1–6, 16–18

Be Grateful

Whiners and naysayers are all around us! For them, the weather is too warm or too cold, the boss is a jerk, and the food is lousy. No matter how good things are, they see only the bad in everything. I invite you to create a complaint-free Lent. This idea is modeled after Maya Angelou's comment, "If you don't like something, change it. If you can't change it, change your attitude. Don't complain."

Embracing a complaint-free Lent begins when we refocus our lives on gratitude. Most of us tend to concentrate so heavily on what's missing in our lives that we barely perceive the good that counterbalances it. When we open up to gratitude, we see clearly how much good there really is. Those things we are lacking are still there, and we still have shortcomings. But instead of focusing on them, we find something to appreciate. I recently spoke with a woman who could only move around in a wheelchair. She said, "My mind is as sharp as ever. I have something to be grateful for."

Gratitude turns denial into acceptance, chaos into order, and confusion into clarity. It can turn a meal into a feast, a house into a home, and a stranger into a friend. Gratitude makes sense of our past, brings peace for today, and creates a vision for tomorrow.

"When you fast, do not look gloomy."
MT 6:16

Work for the Soul » The challenge is to go forty days without complaining. To aid in your effort, wear a rubber band around your wrist. If you find yourself engaging in complaints, gossip, or criticism, snap it. As the days of Lent pass by, you will find yourself doing less complaining and more appreciating.

Words from the Heart » *Dear God, if the only prayer I say is "thank you," that will be enough. Amen.*

February 23 | Thursday after Ash Wednesday
DEUTERONOMY 30:15–20 • LUKE 9:22–25

Born to Bounce Back

Life goes on. The first time I really understood this was the morning after my father died. I opened my eyes to see another beautiful spring day. Clearly, the earth had turned in the night. The sun was shining. Birds were singing. People were talking in the street. I couldn't believe it, but it was true. Life goes on.

In the face of disappointment, disaster, or grief, life goes on, whether we go on or not. Setbacks come in all shapes and sizes and we don't always handle them with ease. Divorce, bankruptcy, cancer, or the death of a loved one—these events have the capacity to crush us forever. They can also redirect us toward the people and things that matter most. So how do we find that gift of really living after experiencing such setbacks?

> *"Take up your cross daily and follow me."*
> LK 9:23

Tap into God's healing power! It gives us the ability to get back up after we've been knocked off our feet. When life throws us a devastating punch, we must express our feelings, deal with our anger or sadness, and face our fears. Once we're in touch with these feelings, with God's help, we can work on releasing them.

Setbacks bring us lessons about life and relationships. If we learn the lesson, we can bounce back and experience stronger personal relationships, clarity about our priorities, and greater personal strength. Then we can find a deeper appreciation for life and emerge from the experience feeling totally alive.

Work for the Soul » Start the day with this bold affirmation: "Go ahead, Life, send me a setback. I eat setbacks for breakfast; they are my fuel for the day!"

Words from the Heart » *Dear God, every now and then life will throw a punch at me. The more I roll with these punches, the easier it is to bounce back! Help me to roll with them. Amen.*

February 24 | Friday after Ash Wednesday
ISAIAH 58:1–9A • MATTHEW 9:14–15

Take Every Opportunity

Only one mourner showed up at the chapel that day—the seventy-six-year-old daughter of the deceased. "Tell me about your father," I said. "He must have been a positive man to have lived so long on his own." "Not really," she said. "He didn't know how to love. Now he's gone and I'm crying for what could have been." As we walked toward the chapel door, she stopped, placed her hand on the casket and said, "Too late!"

We often don't appreciate what we have until it's too late. We leave one job to take on another and then realize how good the old job was. Our kids move away, and we realize how much we miss them. Friends or family members die, and we recognize how precious they were to us.

If we are living with regret, it's time to enter the "no regret" zone, where we can release, refocus, and realize:

1. Release the past for hasty decisions made, adventures missed, and roads not taken;
2. Refocus on life here and now. Remember, tomorrow is not a promise; we only have today;
3. Realize that we'll never have those moments that we missed. We may have time left, though, to say, "I'm sorry," "I love you," "Thank you," or "It's okay."

> "The days will come when the bridegroom is taken away from them."
> MT 9:15

Work for the Soul » Don't put off your dreams for the future. Your "to-do" list might never get done. Right now, no matter what your age, decide who you want to be when you grow up. You have the rest of your life to get it right.

Words from the Heart » *Dear God, help me take advantage of opportunities that come my way so that I may have no room for regrets in my life. Amen.*

February 25 | Saturday after Ash Wednesday
ISAIAH 58:9B–14 • LUKE 5:27–32

Label Jars, Not People

When we label others, we obscure their unique content. People who do this have no idea of the negative impact they have on others. Derogatory labels, which are often based on ignorance and fear, paint individuals with the same brush, thus hiding their uniqueness. After years of counseling, I've observed that those who label others and who continue to speak negatively cause the most damage. Wearing blinders, they can only see from a narrow perspective.

Whenever we receive an unflattering label, our barriers immediately go up. The next time others attempt to label you, take a stand. Say, "Knock it off—your labels are destructive and are not welcome here." It may wake them up and rock their world!

> *"Why do you eat... with the tax collectors and sinners?"*
> LK 5:30

I know someone who believed he was inferior because he only had a sixth-grade education. "I have nothing to offer," he'd say, "because I'm uneducated." Others had given him this label. Fortunately, he's gotten over that. Now, he feels free to share wonderful bits of wisdom with others. Before he was powerless. Now he is confident.

So I propose a label-free Lent. Let's all stop labeling others. Jesus erased labels. He looked beyond the outside appearance to help others see their beauty, richness, and the gifts that made them special. Lent gives us the opportunity to do the same. We can overcome labeling by cultivating unconditional love, compassion, and understanding, and then learn to accept others as they really are.

Work for the Soul » Put a large label on a jar with the words: "Label Jars, Not People." During Lent, every time you label someone, drop a quarter into your jar. At the end of Lent, give the money to your parish or a soup kitchen.

Words from the Heart » *Dear God, help me to see others as you see them: unique and special. Amen.*

February 26 | Sunday, the First Week

GENESIS 2:7–9; 3:1–7 • ROMANS 5:12–19 • MATTHEW 4:1–11

Conquer Your Frustrations

For me, instruction manuals are the ultimate source of frustration. The words: "Assembly Required" cause tightness in my chest and dread in my heart. Life is filled with such emotional triggers: A driver cuts us off on the freeway. A woman darts in front of us at the checkout line. It helps to identify exactly what it is that frustrates us. Many times, we start to blame other non-related things as the source of our frustration and this drains our energy. When we run on depleted energy reserves, we can burn out quickly, and it takes a long time to recover.

Decide to manage your frustrations. Take prayer breaks. Get some exercise. Take a walk. You'll be surprised at how much more resourceful you'll be afterward. Once you've had time to relax and pray, it will be easier to ask yourself some meaningful questions: What is really important to me? What choices do I have? What is my next step? What is the lesson in this experience?

Frustration is an emotional reaction. It doesn't happen "out there." It happens inside and we can choose to entertain it or not. Ninety percent of overcoming the problem is our conscious awareness that it exists. Ask yourself: Three years from now, will this situation be worth the anxiety? Chances are, it won't.

Being able to manage frustration allows us to remain happy and positive even under the most difficult circumstances.

> *"Again the devil took him to a very high mountain and showed him all the kingdoms of the world and their glory."*
> MT 4:8

Work for the Soul » Share your frustrations with an accountability partner. You'll feel better when you speak your mind and find out that the other person may have had a similar experience. He or she could have a helpful suggestion you haven't thought of.

Words from the Heart » *Jesus, please help me accept frustration without getting my buttons pushed. Help me trust you in every situation. Amen.*

February 27 | Monday, the First Week

LEVITICUS 19:1–2, 11–18 • MATTHEW 25:31–46

I Feel Your Pain

"Put yourself in my shoes." It's a familiar request. We say it because we believe that others do not understand how we feel. We'd like for them to identify with us. Empathy is the capacity to understand the feelings of another. It's a special human quality that allows us to step outside of ourselves and see another person from within. Often words are not necessary. Feelings are expressed even when we don't have the ability to describe them.

The realization that, "I, too, may be there one day," is a splendid teacher of empathy. Surely, we can foresee a time when we will face similar obstacles: a negative report from our doctor, an unexpected decrease in our income, a relationship that dissolves rapidly—all of these necessitate a sudden change in priorities.

> "I was hungry, and you gave me something to eat; I was thirsty, and you gave me something to drink; I was a stranger, and you invited me in."
>
> MT 25:35

There are people—right now—who are going through very difficult times. For some, it's a real effort to put one foot in front of the other. This Lent we can enter their world, see their pain, and respond with care and compassion. Or, we can do nothing and be like those people who sit in the window of a fancy restaurant, ignoring the faces of the homeless people looking in.

The day will come when we will need someone to put their arms around us, pray for us, ache with us, and say, "I understand. I've been there."

Work for the Soul » Nobody likes a crisis. We don't know how we'll respond when it happens, so be prepared. Have your "go to" friend's speed dial number. When the worst happens, draw strength from God, who will guide you through the chaos and uncertainty.

Words from the Heart » *Dear God, in times of trouble, I'm hanging on to you. Better yet, I trust that you'll be hanging on to me. Amen.*

February 28 | Tuesday, the First Week

ISAIAH 55:10–11 • MATTHEW 6:7–15

Forgiveness Heals

Few of us make it through life without being hurt by others. When it happens, our emotions can be overwhelming. At first, we may feel anger and resentment. Justice is what we want! And we want the other person to hurt, too.

Do we get over it or get even? Will we heal from the experience or continue to hate? Letting go is not easy. But if we refuse to forgive, we hurt only ourselves. We're not really punishing the other person. They've moved on.

Even if we manage to say, "I forgive you," our hearts can remain locked in resentment. When we continue to hold hostility toward another, we are chained to that person by an emotional link that's stronger than steel. Forgiveness is the only way to break free.

> *"For if you forgive others for their transgressions, your heavenly Father will also forgive you."*
> MT 6:14

It's seldom a one-time process. We have to consciously forgive again and again. One moment we may feel that we've let it go. The next moment, something triggers a painful memory that must be dealt with once more. The deeper we hurt, the more time we need to heal. We've got to let go of the bitterness, so that it no longer consumes us.

Work for the Soul » Try a simple experiment. Make a fist and hold it tight. After a few seconds, you'll start to feel the discomfort. Consider what would happen if your fist remained in this position for weeks, months, or even years. That's what happens with bitterness. The tension is always there. You may want to hurt the other person and get even, but almost without exception, the hurt you do to yourself will be even greater.

Words from the Heart » *Dear God, help me bury the hatchet forever, truly forgive, and be free. Amen.*

March 1 | Wednesday, the First Week

JONAH 3:1–10 • LUKE 11:29–32

Choose a Better Life

Take a look at your life. Is it an endless procession of empty days and restless nights? Do you repeatedly make choices that virtually guarantee your unhappiness? If you answered yes (or even maybe) to these questions, I've got news for you. The power to improve your life is in your hands. You can bounce out of bed each morning eager to face another day filled with opportunities for enjoyment, human contact, and personal growth. Just make the decision to change.

Most of us have played some role in not living the life we want. We carry around extra pounds, display destructive patterns, and cling to unhealthy habits. We fail to make the most of our talents, fight with those we care about, and collapse emotionally from upsetting events.

> *"They repented at the preaching of Jonah."*
> LK 11:32

It's our choice. We can choose patterns that defeat ourselves or actions that affirm and honor ourselves. Most people decide to conquer their self-defeating behavior when they hit rock bottom. In the throes of despair, they decide: "No more!"

Practice repetition. Experts say that it takes twenty-one days for a change in behavior to become a habit and a minimum of six months for the practice to become ingrained into your daily life. Begin your positive, affirming habits now.

Work for the Soul » On an index card, write down your self-defeating behavior and the price you pay for engaging in it. List the opportunities you have missed because you chose these actions. Now begin to choose healthier alternatives. Put the index card into an envelope, address it to yourself, and mail it in three weeks. Then, contemplate and marvel at how far you've come.

Words from the Heart » *Dear God, I need your help to change my behavior and reclaim my power. I promise to do my part. Amen.*

March 2 | Thursday, the First Week

ESTHER C:12, 14–16, 23–25 • MATTHEW 7:7–12

Three Magic Words

A priest was handling a funeral service at a local cemetery. As they were leaving, the husband of the deceased leaned over and hugged the casket. He turned to the priest and said, "Father, I loved my wife." The priest answered, "I know, Paul. It's time to leave." The man paused for a moment, looked longingly at the casket and said, "Father, I really loved my wife, and one day I almost told her so."

If I could get every person in the world to include three words in their vocabulary, they would be, "I love you." No other words have as much power to heal or move a relationship forward. These three words are so critical, yet many of us take them for granted. One thing is for certain: no one ever gets tired of hearing them. Without receiving them in a consistent dose, a soul will start to wither. When we express these words, we are saying, "I'm so lucky to have you," and "You're the one person on this planet I want to spend my life with."

The poet W.H. Auden remarked, "We must love one another or die!" He's so right. Our relationships cannot survive without verbal expressions of love. The phrase, "there's no time like the present, " applies here without question. Start now!

> *"Ask, and it will be given to you; seek, and you will find; knock, and it will be opened to you."*
>
> MT 7:7

Work for the Soul » Try saying "I love you" when it's least expected. If your spouse is used to hearing you express your love when you leave for work in the morning, call again when you get to the office. Pray, during Lent, that the Lord will increase your love to overflowing. Happy Valentine's Day!

Words from the Heart » *Dear God, You are always there to catch me when I fall and listen when I need to talk. I love you! Amen.*

March 3 | Friday, the First Week

EZEKIEL 18:21–18 • MATTHEW 5:20–26

Resolve to Reconcile

Caroline came to see me three weeks after her father died of a heart attack. She was away when it happened and was devastated by the news. They had a heated argument two days before he died and harsh words had been spoken. She was regretful for things said and unsaid. "What did you argue about? I asked. "Something stupid," she replied.

Unfinished business can be major, such as a bitter rivalry among siblings, family secrets that were never shared, or important matters that remain unresolved. It could be a child who has not spoken to his or her parents in years, a spouse who dies suddenly during a crisis, or a last will and testament that was never completed.

More often, less dramatic events cause misunderstandings: A mother may still feel guilty about punishing her daughter, a wife may not have forgiven her husband, or a son may believe that his parents loved his brother more. In Caroline's case, a daughter was disappointed that her father died before they could be reconciled. These memories can be overwhelming for the person left to grieve.

> *"Go first and be reconciled with your brother, and then come and offer your gift."*
> MT 5:24

Unfinished business deprives us of a sense of peace. It seems final. We've lost our last chance to work through old issues or to tell someone how we really feel.

Work for the Soul » If you still live with haunting memories, nagging resentments or even anger, consider talking to a trusted friend, priest, or grief counselor so you can process your feelings. Seek to gain closure. Talk it out. Don't leave things unsaid that need to be said. Resolve to reconcile with your past so you can move on with your life.

Words from the Heart » *Dear God, you understand the sorrow of unfinished business. Help me work through mine so I that I may find peace again. Amen.*

March 4 | Saturday, the First Week

DEUTERONOMY 26:16–19 • MATTHEW 5:43–48

Love Your Enemies

It's human nature to want to retaliate when we're attacked or offended. How we respond, however, is a matter of choice. When a spouse betrays, a friend abandons, or an employer cheats, we keep score.

Jesus offered us a different approach: loving our enemies. Can he be serious? Or, are his words meant only for people like Gandhi or Mother Teresa? Love your enemies. That's it! Love them even if it's not easy. Jesus was serious when he gave this command. He knew that it would be difficult for us, yet it is something we must do.

Why? Because our enemies are children of God, just like us. To love our enemies doesn't mean that we should neglect to respect ourselves or that we should allow people to do violence to us or to others. It just means not to harbor hatred in our hearts. Jesus was a perfect example. Even as they crucified him, he loved them.

> *"Love your enemies and pray for those who persecute you."*
> MT 5:44

We have a choice—to hate or to love. With love, we find ways to soothe and slowly heal our wounds. Only love enables us to separate a person from his or her actions. Love is caring and compassionate. It lets go of what was done or said, and helps us understand what motivated the unkind behavior in the first place. With love, we can see the world through the other person's eyes and be free from the anger and revenge that enslave us.

Work for the Soul » If you have said or done something offensive to someone, apologize. Ask for forgiveness. Look for opportunities to share a kind word, shake a hand, or offer love.

Words from the Heart » *Dear God, give me great patience and confidence as I attempt to love those who are not very lovable. It isn't easy, but with your help, I can do it. Amen.*

March 5 | Sunday, the Second Week

GENESIS 12:1–4A • 2 TIMOTHY 1:8B–10 • MATTHEW 17:1–9

Define Your Moment

Elizabeth was rushed to the emergency room after suffering a severe stroke. Her husband, Michael, who had Alzheimer's disease, had been her entire life. She bathed and clothed him. She cooked and sang Italian operas to him. She only left him on Thursdays to buy groceries and on Sundays to attend services. But this time, she didn't come home.

When her son Patrick arrived at the hospital, he found her in intensive care. We sat down to talk frankly about the prognosis. There was little hope of recovery. After praying with me, Patrick left to break the news to his father.

When he arrived at the house, he noticed a letter on the kitchen table addressed to him. He opened it and read, "Dear Patrick, if you are reading this letter, I'm either dead or so sick that I can't take care of myself. I've never asked you for anything, but now I need your help. Promise me you'll take care of Dad. Please, I need your promise. I love you. Mom."

"And he was transfigured before them; and his face shone like the sun."
MT 17:2

That evening, Patrick leaned over his mother's bedside and whispered, "Mom, I promise to take care of Dad. I love you." Later that evening, Elizabeth died.

There are defining moments of transformation in everyone's life, times when we clearly see what is most important and what has eternal value. We're never quite the same afterward.

Work for the Soul » What was your defining moment? It's helpful to review your life in stages (childhood, adolescence, adulthood, elder years), and write down your thoughts and memories. Ask yourself: What was my defining moment and how did it change my life?

Words from the Heart » *Dear God, I will always cherish those special moments that opened up unlimited possibilities for me to remember and to love. Amen.*

March 6 | Monday, the Second Week

DANIEL 9:4B-10 • LUKE 6:36-38

Live without Judgment

When the happy couple exchanged wedding vows, Melissa's family and friends thought: What could she possibly see in him? Nick had massive arms covered with tattoos. He rode a motorcycle and wore leather and the usual biker attire. Melissa was completely turned off by him at first. After all, he was different and didn't fit in with her lifestyle. It was only after she got to know him that she discovered his intelligence, respectfulness, and kindness. He was definitely someone she wanted to spend the rest of her life with.

All too often, we make quick judgments that should be reconsidered. We don't have to love everyone we meet or be friends with everyone, but we do at least have to give them a chance. Sometimes, we are quick to judge others by the way they dress, their job, how they wear their hair, their age, or any number of reasons that keep us from seeing, hearing, or appreciating the person in front of us.

> *"Do not judge and you will not be judged."*
> LK 6:37

Try living without judgment. Go into a new situation without preconceived notions or ideas. Have an open mind with no requirements, conditions, or expectations. Follow the advice of this American Indian proverb: "Do not judge your neighbor until you walk two moons in his moccasins." We just might begin to see things that we've never seen before.

Work for the Soul » Every person has value. Lent is a great time to see people through the eyes of Jesus. Think about the people you know who are often passed over, forgotten, judged, or quickly dismissed. Take time this week to get to know them. Do something special for them.

Words from the Heart » *Dear God, please forgive me if I have been quick to judge others. Help me discover those rich opportunities to grow closer to them. Amen.*

March 7 | Tuesday, the Second Week

ISAIAH 1:10, 16–20 • MATTHEW 23:1–12

Learn from Role Models

I have benefited greatly from various role models in my life: preachers who have impacted my style, scholars who have changed my way of thinking, writers who have inspired my own writing, and pastors who have influenced the way I serve.

Role models come into our lives and enrich our experience. They give us advice, coaching, encouragement, and support. They are the parents, friends, neighbors, and teachers whom we honor and cherish. They both inquire and inspire.

Role models inquire. They keep learning. A person can have all kinds of talent but if they aren't willing to learn from others, they will never advance or increase their knowledge. They are eager to learn anything that will help them improve. They ask questions and listen.

Role models inspire. They consistently live by what they believe. They seek to align their lives with God's Word. They live the same lives at church and at home, in public and in private. They reveal their sincerity by the way they give their time, resources, and compassion to those around them. They show love toward others in the way they talk, the forgiveness they extend, and the consideration they show.

> *"Do not do what they do, for they do not practice what they preach."*
> MT 23:3

They're intimately interested in our spiritual and psychological well-being. They assist us in building confidence and character. They elevate us and offer steady, consistent advice over the long haul.

Work for the Soul » Who are your role models? What family members, teachers, or friends have had an impact on you? Share with them how they have influenced your life. Send them a note of appreciation and gratitude.

Words from the Heart » *Dear God, as I live out my Christian life, I will do so carefully. Others may be watching me as their role model. May my actions speak louder than my words. Amen.*

March 8 | Wednesday, the Second Week

JEREMIAH 18:18–20 • MATTHEW 20:17–28

Practice Acts of Kindness

When I was in the eighth grade, one of the girls in my class had a deformity that caused one of her legs to be shorter than the other. She also had a weight problem and didn't socialize well with the other students. Rather than befriend her, most of my classmates tormented her. I don't recall that I ever said anything to her directly, but I'm sure I laughed at the jokes (which weren't funny) and I certainly did nothing to make her feel that she had a friend. To this day, I can remember what we called her, but I can't remember her name. I wish now that I could beg her for forgiveness.

The greatest hindrances to joy are the scars that come from the bullies of life. Even if we do not commit the abuse, we are complicit if we say nothing and allow it to happen. This behavior shows a lack of respect, not only for the person involved, but for God who created this person as a beloved spiritual child.

Be kind and thoughtful rather than aggressive and cruel. Refuse to associate with those who ridicule others. Speak to the person involved and offer your friendship, encouragement, and support. Adopt the example of Jesus, and pray that others will notice your behavior and follow your example.

> *"You know that the rulers of the Gentiles lord it over them, and their high officials exercise authority over them. It can't be that way with you."*
> MT 20:25–26

Work for the Soul » This Lent, pick up after yourself so no one else has to. Let someone go in front of you in line. Refuse to criticize another. Be friendly to someone who is alone, and listen carefully when another person speaks.

Words from the Heart » *Dear God, help me be kind and gentle in little ways so I can be considerate and helpful with bigger things. Amen.*

March 9 | Thursday of the Second Week

JEREMIAH 17:5–10 • LUKE 16:19–31

Live Like You Were Dying

When his wife and son arrived at the emergency room, he was already dead. She was in complete shock. The child kept crying, "Daddy, wake up. Please wake up." His father had left for work that morning, told his boss he didn't feel well, sat down for a minute, and then passed out. When the paramedics arrived, it was too late. He had gone into cardiac arrest and couldn't be revived.

Death changes families forever. It also teaches us that being "alive" is a fantastic gift. Too many people grumble about their everyday lives. Few fill their time with the art of actually "living." The key is to learn how to let go of the darkness and experience more of the brighter side of life.

I am determined to be fully engaged in my life and not just go through the motions. I may move more slowly, but I'm determined to move. I may not be able to eat as much, but I refuse to relinquish the joy of food. I may develop limitations, but I'm determined to keep my eyes and ears wide open, to make room for every new experience.

> *"'No, father Abraham,' he said, 'but if someone from the dead goes to them, they will repent.'"*
> LK 16:30

Push your own "go" button and get started. Make time count. Ask yourself: What are my priorities? What is really important to me? What do I value most? The gift of the present is this precious moment before us. Use it wisely. Start living!

Work for the Soul » Listen to Tim McGraw's song: "Live Like You Were Dying." Share with family and friends how the music and words touched you and challenged you to take nothing for granted.

Words from the Heart » *Dear God, when I wake up, it's a new day loaded with possibilities and opportunities. I don't ever want to waste this precious time. Amen.*

March 10 | Friday, the Second Week

GENESIS 37:3–4, 12–13A, 17B–28A • MATTHEW 21:33–43, 45–46

Who Is Our God?

In the movie *Bruce Almighty*, a young man (Jim Carrey) experiences life as series of bitter disappointments. He's fed up with calling on God and not getting the relief he wants from his chaotic life. Enter God (Morgan Freeman). He temporarily hands over his divine powers to Bruce to teach him a loving lesson about greed, desire, power, and "having it all." This is the kind of healthy image of God that we all need in our lives.

Lent is a marvelous time to toss out distorted images of God that we have carried around in the past, like the "Truth or Consequences" God: we tell the truth or pay the consequences; the "Santa Claus" God: we're on his list and he's passing judgment; the "Deal or No Deal" God: when life deals us a blow, we bargain with God.

We cannot have twisted, uncaring images and have a wholesome relationship with God. Instead, we need to reconnect with the God who delights in us, who appreciates, enjoys, values, and cherishes us as unique individuals.

> *"The kingdom of God will be taken away from you and given to a people that produces the fruits of the kingdom."*
> MT 21:43

God offers us love—unconditionally, completely, and absolutely. We can't win this love, lose it, or even earn it. We can, however, refuse it. The choice is ours. I love this quote: "God loves me just as I am, but God also loves me too much to let me stay the way I am." Lent is the ideal time for God to stir within us a desire to improve and become better persons.

Work for the Soul » Write down on paper a description of your old images of God. Then burn the paper. Create (and carry with you) healthy, positive, and life-affirming images of God.

Words from the Heart » *Dear God, when I am quiet, I can hear your gentle voice whisper, "You are special." Thank you for never giving up on me. Amen.*

March 11 | Saturday, the Second Week

MICAH 7:14–15, 18–20 • LUKE 15:1–3, 11–32

Spiritual Amnesia

Jean's voice had an edge to it. She was extremely upset. As our phone conversation unfolded, I discovered deep emotional wounds that were fueling her anger. She was raised in a religious home. Her stepfather was involved in the local parish but behind closed doors he was a different man. There were beatings, emotional abuse, and even threats against her life. As a young teen, Jean ran away from her home, her church, and even from God.

One thing that hinders our growth is the baggage from our past. We remember words that we regret and relationships that failed. There are people around us who dig up the past, dump it on us, and rob us of our peace. But we must understand that they can only do this if they have our permission! Find new supportive friends to spend time with.

> *"This brother of yours was dead and has come to life; he was lost and has been found."*
> LK 15:32

Focus on thoughts that empower you and help you feel better and make the decision to reconcile with your past. Letting go empowers us to be responsible for our lives and our choices. Perhaps one day, we can finally release the painful past, as Jean did.

She caught a glimpse of a billboard that changed her life forever. In big, bold letters, it read: "Forget the former things, don't dwell on the past." It was an old message, but this time, it caused a shift in her consciousness.

Work for the Soul » What do you keep turning up in your memory that causes fear, hurt, worry, or anxiety? Find someone to talk to. Replace the painful memories with gratefulness for your life, and marvel as you attract more of the things that you are grateful for.

Words from the Heart » *Dear God, I've made some choices that I'm not proud of. Thank you for giving me a clean slate and the opportunity to begin again. Amen.*

March 12 | Sunday, the Third Week

EXODUS 17:3–7 • ROMANS 5:1–2, 5–8 • JOHN 4:5–42

Keep Your Nicks to Yourself

Rapunzel was a beautiful young woman with long, lovely hair. According to the fairy tale, a mean old witch told her she was ugly and locked her in a castle. By believing the witch, she felt inferior, inadequate, and intimidated.

Words are powerful. They can hurt or heal, build up or tear down, comfort or curse. Those little put-downs that we carelessly throw out can leave scars on someone's self-esteem.

Some people excuse "nicking" as just being honest. But they don't realize that their words can be devastating. Their friends may have had to pick up the pieces after a vicious rumor was spread. Or perhaps, they spent time recovering from the hurt of being called a "loser." To these people, nicks may be far from funny!

> *"Many of the Samaritans from that town believed in him because of the woman's testimony."*
>
> JN 4:39

Choose words that empower! You can boost someone's confidence with an encouraging word at just the right moment. With the power of your voice, you can reach out, minister to, and encourage others.

Be immaculate with your words, and speak like Jesus did with the woman at the well. He spoke the truth while communicating a soothing acceptance, making her feel loved and valued. When we are flawless with our words, we only use them in the direction of truth and love. And even though we make this promise, we may slip up on occasion. When this happens, we acknowledge it, apologize, and move on.

Work for the Soul » Take this pledge: I pledge to be more aware of the words I use. I will become conscious of how gossip hurts people (including myself) and eliminate it from my life. Every week, I will say this pledge with my family and friends.

Words from the Heart » *Dear God, may my words always be gentle and tender so that they may help, heal, and give joy to others. Amen.*

March 13 | Monday, the Third Week

2 KINGS 5:1–15AB • LUKE 4:24–30

When You Get Angry, SING

Almost everyone gets angry. Yes, even mild-mannered people (like me), lose their cool or hit the roof occasionally. Sometimes anger can be good. For example, when we are treated unfairly, anger can be the motivator we need to help us stand up for ourselves. But anger must be released in a safe way. Otherwise, it's like a pot of boiling water with the lid left on. When it gets out of control, it can lead to problems at work, in personal relationships, and in the overall quality of our lives.

I would like to suggest that we use the acronym "SING" to safely release our anger. It's easy to remember:

Stop and notice your symptoms when you get angry. Look for the signs.

Imagine the consequences if you lose control. If we try to picture the consequences, it can help us engage our brain before we snap.

Notice what you really get angry about. What are your triggers? What pushes your buttons?

Get away from the source. Often, our anger is so intense that we can't solve the problem until we cool down. Ask yourself: What can I do to reduce my anger? Take a few moments to discuss this with God, then take a walk or a soothing shower. Try to relax.

Life is filled with frustrating moments and the unpredictable actions of others. We can't change those events, but we can change the way we react to them.

> *"All of the people in the synagogue were furious when they heard this."*
> LK 4:28

Work for the Soul » Carry a small stone in your pocket. When you start to feel irritation, keep moving the pebble from one pocket to the other. This will help interrupt the anger cycle and give you a chance to regroup.

Words from the Heart » *Dear God, when I start to get angry, help me walk away before I say or do something that I'll regret. Amen.*

March 14 | Tuesday, the Third Week

DANIEL 3:25, 34–43 • MATTHEW 18:21–35

We All Need Patience

Standing in the bank line, I could feel the frustration mounting. The lone teller was taking her time with a hearing-impaired customer and kept repeating herself. Those waiting with me rolled their eyes, exchanged glances, and sighed.

Arnold H. Glasgow once wrote: "The key to everything is patience." It's a virtue that's hard to practice in a society that measures time in nanoseconds. As the speed of our lives increases, our patience seems to decrease. We're so used to rapid response times and quick fixes that we get upset when things don't go our way or when we have to wait for something.

Patience requires that we slow down and be present to whatever is happening around us. I have found that patience can be learned by practicing "five and ten."

> *"Be patient with me, and I will pay you back."*
> MT 18:29

For one week (five minutes each day), decide not to let anything bother you. If a situation arises that tests your patience, notice what happens. If your mind starts racing with all sorts of quick fixes, just observe the thoughts and let them float by. You don't have to act on them and there is no rush to fix anything.

In the second week, expand this exercise to ten minutes a day. Choose times that often test your patience: during rush-hour traffic, waiting in lines, or any activity that requires a delay. As you continue this practice, you'll find that you will be able to respond to life's obstacles and challenges with a greater sense of strength, focus, and inner peace.

Work for the Soul » Share the "five and ten" exercise with someone you know who is having a difficult time with patience.

Words from the Heart » *Dear God, I want to become so good at practicing patience that it becomes my natural state of being. Amen.*

March 15 | Wednesday, the Third Week

DEUTERONOMY 4:1, 5–9 • MATTHEW 5:17–19

Nothing but the Truth

When the teacher discovered that someone had cheated on the exam, she confronted the class and outlined the consequences. Later that day, an embarrassed young man tearfully said, "It was me." In the world of the little white lie, the half-truth and shaded reality, it is refreshing to find an individual who will come forward and accept blame for his wrongdoing. When we're caught doing something we shouldn't be doing, it's so easy to lie about it. The police officer stops us and asks, "Do you know how fast you were going?" and we say, "I didn't realize I was speeding." Your spouse asks if you made that important phone call. You respond, "I tried, but the line was busy."

"I tell you the truth."
MT 5:18

If we lie, the consequences over time are often far more destructive and painful than the conflict that the lie was meant to avoid. Be completely honest. Speak the truth. Tell the absolute, complete truth, no matter what!

When the boss praises you for work you didn't do, be honest. When your coworker gets raked over the coals for a mistake you made, speak up and admit that it was your fault. When you have offended someone through insensitivity or harsh remarks, don't deny it. Ask for forgiveness. Promise to do better.

Jesus calls us to a more noble way of life. Our lives should be the epitome of integrity. Just the truth! Give it a try! After all, for the Christian, honesty is not just the best policy; it's the only policy!

Work for the Soul » "Our lives are shaped by the significant truths we say or don't say." Print this statement and pass it along to others. Leave it at work, in church pews, and at store counters. It will catch on.

Words from the Heart » *Dear God, you know the truth about me, so being honest really carries no risk. The truth may startle me, but it delights you. Amen.*

March 16 | Thursday, the Third Week

JEREMIAH 7:23–28 • LUKE 11:14–23

Say Nothing at All

After an eight-year battle with leukemia, his seventeen-year-old daughter was laid to rest. Many people offered their condolences: "She suffered so long, it's a blessing." "She's in a much better place." These words, though well intended, did nothing to ease his loss. Soon after the funeral, a neighbor stopped by to see him. She didn't launch into a litany of platitudes. Instead, she just sat with him and held his hand. The grief-stricken man later said: "It was such a comfort, I wish she had stayed all day."

I will tell you a secret. Helping those who are hurting or brokenhearted can be summarized in two words: Be there! You really don't need to say anything. Accept all emotion, suspend all judgment, and resist the tendency to give advice or fix the problem.

> *"He who is not with me is against me."*
> LK 11:23

You might not know exactly what to say, but that's all right. You don't have to have all the answers. When in doubt, be silent and give emotional support. Don't feel pressured to fill the silence with chatter.

Allow the person to voice anger or sadness. A squeeze of the hand, a hug, or a smile can be the best pain reliever. If you feel the need to say something, "I'm sorry" or "I care" will be more than enough. Have confidence in the power of simply being there.

Work for the Soul » If you have a friend who is going through a difficult time, invite him or her over for dinner. Call, write a card, or send a short note. Be there as long as it takes. This helps the person look forward to your presence without asking for help again and again.

Words from the Heart » *Dear God, I know when pain is fresh, my words should be few. Just showing up lets a friend know that I care. Amen.*

March 17 | Friday, the Third Week
HOSEA 14:2–10 • MARK 12:28–34

Embrace the Darkness

Life can be sailing along smoothly, and then all of a sudden—BOOM!—the bottom falls out! We lose a job, feel our health deteriorate, or watch a relationship crumble. At times like these, we can be troubled, discouraged, and ready to throw in the towel.

Many of us have experienced times like these. It may be the circumstances of life that bring us down: an accident or illness, betrayal by a friend, or the loss of a loved one. And sometimes, we have no idea why we're so depressed.

These difficulties might just be the wake-up calls that we need to change or make something right in our lives. But we don't have to sit alone and be lost in the darkness. We have choices. Recovery and counseling programs can help us grow, adjust to new circumstances, manage an addiction, or even motivate us to change the direction of our lives.

"Love the Lord your God with all your heart..."
MK 12:30

When you experience such a period in your life, talk to a friend, especially someone who knows what it's like (who's been through it) so that he or she can offer support as it unfolds. By talking to someone, you'll gain perspective regarding what you can expect along the way.

Look at the darkness directly, spend time with it, embrace it, and trust that it comes with a lesson. That's when you can learn from the experience.

Work for the Soul » If you have friends who are going through a dark period in their lives, reach out to them. Offer your support. Give them your friendship and this quote: "Don't turn your head. Keep looking at the bandaged place. That's where the light is."

Words from the Heart » *Dear God, when it's darkest, the stars come out. May the stars guide me to a safe place. Amen.*

March 18 | Saturday, the Third Week

HOSEA 6:1–6 • LUKE 18:9–14

"Mistake" Anxiety!

A federal employee was upset when she received her performance review. Her evaluator wrote, "When she opens her mouth, it's only to change whatever foot was previously in there."

A strong statement of judgment perhaps, but I can definitely relate to that employee. I sometimes make a mistake, and the next thing I know, I've made it again! We all make mistakes. But what's different about each of us is how we handle them. Some of us get angry and upset, others take it in stride, and still others are simply in denial—Mistake? What mistake?

Whenever I read the parable of the tax collector and the Pharisee at the temple, I ask myself: Who would I be sitting next to and identifying with? That's not hard to figure out—the tax collector! I'd ask him to move over, sit in his place, and say: "God, I failed again." And God would respond: "So what? It's not the end of the world. The earth will still be in orbit and the mosquitoes will still be biting."

> *"The tax collector stood at a distance and said, 'God, have mercy on me, a sinner.'"*
> LK 18:13

In many cases, mistakes can be our best teachers because they require that we learn vital lessons. They call for us to stop and consider our circumstances carefully, right here, right now. Aldous Huxley (English novelist and critic), sums it up best: "Experience is not what happens to you. It's what you do with what happens to you."

Work for the Soul » When you (or someone you know) keep agonizing over an error made, read Matthew 11:29–30, and then turn all of your burdens over to Jesus.

Words from the Heart » *Dear God, if people can't accept my imperfections, it's their problem, not mine. Amen.*

March 19 | Sunday, the Fourth Week

1 SAMUEL 16:1B, 6–7, 10–13A • EPHESIANS 5:8–14 • JOHN 9:1–41

Live for Today

When life is ripped apart, and all the things that matter most are gone in an instant, we ask: Why? Why me? What have I done to bring this into my life? There are no answers to why bad things happen. The question should be: When bad things happen, what can we do? We can isolate ourselves, become angry with everyone and never move on, or we can turn our pain over to God and welcome new experiences into our lives.

When Kevin was diagnosed with stage 2 colon cancer, the doctors told him he had only four months to live. That was over three years ago. Kevin is a single father of three teenage children. He works full time and receives chemotherapy every couple of weeks. I asked him, "How do you live each day with cancer hanging over your head?" He smiled and said, "I treat every day as an adventure, and I refuse to let anything make me sad, angry, or worried. I live for today. Believe it or not, I'm happier now than I was before I was diagnosed."

> *"Rabbi, who sinned, this man or his parents, that he was born blind?"*
> JN 9:2

We all have to cope with the painful and unfair circumstances. It's fair and healthy to ask "Why?" However, I've seen too many people hang on to that question far too long. Kevin is not sitting with his head in his hands, asking, "Why me?" He's living his life. We should be living our lives as well!

Work for the Soul » If you ever wondered whether you should intrude on someone's sorrow, the answer is: "Yes—you must." Your friends need your help and will feel even more rejected if you don't call, write, or sit with them during the difficult times.

Words from the Heart » *Dear God, when I'm in pain, help me feel better, see things differently, and be open to new possibilities. Amen.*

March 20 | Joseph, Husband of Mary

2 SAMUEL 7:4–5A, 12–14A, 16 • ROMANS 4:13, 16–18, 22 • MATTHEW 1:16, 18–21, 24A OR LUKE 2:41–51A

The Price You Pay

"It's not supposed to be this way," the father of a dying teenager cried. "I wasn't supposed to live longer than my son." When you bury a child, you're faced with reconstructing your life. The place you reserved in the center of your heart for your unique son or daughter is now aching.

Most parents feel a sense of guilt and blame themselves for the tragedy. They should never have let the child drive, backpack, or swim. Whether the death occurred suddenly or after a long illness, the parents may torture themselves with thoughts that they should have done something different. Perhaps suffering could have been reduced or death avoided altogether.

> *"When Joseph awoke from sleep, he did as the angel of the Lord commanded him."* MT 1:24

Everyone grieves differently. There is no timetable. Avoid being with people who cannot honor your feelings of despair, sadness, longing, or regret. You have lost a loved one, and you need to talk to others who have been through the same experience. Talk openly about your loved one's life and your strongest emotions. The support, comfort, and understanding gained through this interaction can be profound.

It may take many months (perhaps years) to weave this traumatic experience into your life and move on. You'll eventually be able to resume social activities and perhaps even go on a vacation again. Inevitably, you will change and have a different perspective on what you feel is important.

Work for the Soul » Begin a project that you can work on quietly, slowly, and lovingly: a scrapbook of photos, a letter or poem to your loved one, or a piece of prose that describes your feelings. Write down everything this person meant to you and recap those special moments often.

Words from the Heart » *Dear God, when a loved one dies, it's so tough! I need to feel your love through the care of others who have been there. Amen.*

March 21 | Tuesday, the Fourth Week

EZEKIEL 47:1–9, 12 • JOHN 5:1–16

Choose Your Words Wisely

Cynics will say that using positive affirmations is nonsense and that only the naive would believe in it. Yet, we create our experience all the time, with everything we think, say, believe, feel, and do, whether we are conscious of it or not.

An affirmation is a verbal or written statement that is used repeatedly to help redesign your life. The words chosen should be positive, in the present tense, and make you feel good when you hear them. Always focus on the feeling or outcome that you desire. Affirmations take time to be effective and can eventually help counter the negative traits that many of us affirm on a daily basis.

"Get up! Pick up your mat and walk."

JN 5:8

Start using positive affirmations to change your negative self-talk. Here are some examples: I am what I choose to be; I am special; today is a new day; I learn from my mistakes; I can handle it; Life is God's gift to me; God loves me.

It's important that the positive affirmations we select resonate with us and feel natural and appropriate. The stronger our connection with the words, the deeper the impression they make on us, the sooner we will experience positive results.

Work for the Soul » Create your own list of positive affirmations. Tape them to your mirror. Keep them in your desk drawer, wallet, or purse or use them as the background on your computer screen. Then, when negative thoughts start to creep in, take out your affirmations, read them, and start to feel good again.

Words from the Heart » *Dear God, I can always count on your words and your love to build me up and make me feel better. Amen.*

March 22 | Wednesday, the Fourth Week

ISAIAH 49:8–15 • JOHN 5:17–30

Nothing Lasts Forever

The church was crowded with family and friends who were stunned, angry, and bitter that a drunk driver could snuff out a life so suddenly. As the liturgy progressed, husbands and wives who had entered the building separately, moved closer, embraced and cried. Children who had raced in ahead of their parents were now being cuddled and held.

Death can definitely bring people together. It reminds us that we don't have forever and if we're going to make our statement, express our love, or experience life, it must be done now. Death has no respect for age, social status, or economic level. It comes to us all.

I've learned so much from those who have died before me. They've taught me that there's no holding on, that we must let go, and that there's nothing wrong with parting tears or the pain of mourning. Every hello is the beginning of a new goodbye. Nothing is permanent. The time for life is now!

It's not death that we should fear. Rather, the real tragedy is the possibility of a life not lived. The more we understand this, the easier we will come to accept death and the more fully we'll be able to live life here and now.

> "The Father raises the dead and gives them life."
> JN 5:21

Work for the Soul » If someone close to you has died, you may be sad, worried, or scared. You might feel angry, guilty, or just plain empty. Even if you don't feel like talking, find ways to express your emotions. Start writing in a journal about the memories you have of the person who died and how you've been feeling since the loss.

Words from the Heart » *Dear God, the day I was born, you promised that my life would have meaning. Help me learn to cherish every moment. Amen.*

March 23 | Thursday, the Fourth Week

EXODUS 32:17–14 • JOHN 5:31–47

Star in Your Own Life!

Dan constantly worries about what others think of him. In an effort to please his boss, he agrees to take on too many tasks and then gets stuck staying late at work. He gets so tired of living up to other people's expectations that he just wants to scream: "Hey, I am what I am and if you don't like it, tough."

We all enjoy getting the approval of others, but let's not bend ourselves into a pretzel to get them to like us. If we get their approval, that's fine; if we don't, we'll survive.

Lent is a good time to cure the "disease to please." It's easy to spot the symptoms—that blank look on our face when we're asked what we want, that panic sensation we sense when someone dislikes us, the resentment we feel when we have to do things we don't want to do for others.

> *"I don't accept praise from people."*
> JN 5:41

Here's the cure:

Me-time: Schedule time away from your job, spouse, and children. Use this opportunity to tune in to what you really need and want.

No-time: Break the yes habit by saying: no. It gets easier with practice. Try it in front of the mirror. Practice it in phrases, such as: "No, I can't do that," or "No, I don't want to go there."

Truth-time: Be who you are! We are responsible for speaking what we perceive to be the truth, not what others want to hear.

Work for the Soul » Plan a day to pamper yourself. When someone tries to get you to do something else, politely say: "No, I have other plans." Do whatever feels wonderful for you!

Words from the Heart » *Dear God, before the "disease to please" becomes fatal in my life, give me the courage to speak out for what I need and want. Amen.*

March 24 | Friday, the Fourth Week
WISDOM 2:1A, 12–22 • JOHN 7:1–2, 10, 25–30

This Too Shall Pass!

A king once asked his jeweler to design a special ring with a unique inscription, appropriate for difficult times. When it arrived, the king was very pleased. It read, "This too shall pass!" Adversity will not last forever. What will last is our ability to survive. When we face hard times, we often panic, turn away from those we love, act out of desperation, make unwise decisions, and say things that we later regret.

Our ability to cope is affected by our personality, our support system, and the severity of the setback. There is no sure-fire formula for bouncing back from adversity. However, there are three steps you can take to make the process easier.

> *"No one laid a hand on him, because his time had not yet come."*
> JN 7:30

1. Always find someone to talk to. Don't try to go through it by yourself. It's a long road when we try to face tough times alone.
2. Believe everything will turn out all right. Say out loud every day, "Let not my heart be troubled or afraid" (Jn 14:1). Tomorrow always comes. Tough times don't last, but tough people do.
3. Cast aside all worry. It's time to stop stewing and start doing. Focus on what needs to be changed, look for new opportunities, and then get to work.

When the Japanese mend broken objects, they fill the cracks with gold. They believe that when something (with history) has suffered damage, it becomes stronger and more beautiful. So will we.

Work for the Soul » Create wristbands with the phrase, "This too shall pass." Make the bands yellow, the color of hope. Distribute them to people in your parish, neighborhood, or place of employment.

Words from the Heart » *Dear God, sometimes I don't handle struggles and disappointments very well. Replace my panic with the peace of knowing that everything will be okay. Amen.*

March 25 | Annunciation of the Lord
ISAIAH 7:10–14; 8:10 • HEBREWS 10:4–10 • LUKE 1:26–38

Lend Me Your Ears

I cannot imagine what it would be like to be deaf—to miss the sound of the wind blowing through the trees, the birds chirping at dawn and the words "I love you." While I can't imagine that silent experience, I can say, with regret, that I don't always listen to those things that I am able to hear. During conversation, my mind sometimes wanders, or I'll be busy preparing my answer, instead of listening. I'm not the only one. Many of us are great at talking, but few of us are skilled at listening.

Listening demonstrates love. In relationships, we want to be able to convey our doubts, fears, dreams, and passions. We long for these things to be embraced by those we share them with. We want to feel confident that we will be heard, not judged, blamed, or interrupted. Listening provides comfort, recognition, and understanding of our thoughts, feelings, and emotions.

> "Nothing is impossible with God."
> LK 1:37

Tweak your listening skills by focusing on the other person. People usually talk to feel understood, not to get advice. Repeat back what you think you heard to avoid any misunderstanding.

Don't judge or dismiss the person's experience or perspective. It's okay to tell the person that you don't have the answer. Remember, when you listen, you give the greatest gift, the gift of caring.

Work for the Soul » Listening is half of communication. When you talk, you want others to understand your perspective. Just make sure they know that you understand theirs. You do that by listening. Use an egg timer to improve your skills. Turn it to the maximum amount of time and don't speak a word until it goes off.

Words from the Heart » *Dear God, prayer works so well because you don't tell me how to feel or give me advice, you listen and then whisper the words I need to hear. Amen.*

March 26 | Sunday, the Fifth Week
EZEKIEL 37:12–14 • ROMANS 8:8–11 • JOHN 11:1–45

Open Your Heart

I sat with James, whose mother was on life support. He kept trying to hold back the tears. "I have to be strong for my brother," he said. I told him, "No, you don't. It hurts. Get it out!"

It's unhealthy when we hold back tears. We are meant to experience and express our emotions fully. There's nothing as healing as a good cry. Tears are a gesture of compassion. A tear falling on a casket says what a spoken word could not. What summons a mother's compassion and concern more quickly than a tear on a child's cheek?

What receives more support and sympathy than a tear on the face of a friend? Our tears are the sign that we've taken the focus from ourselves, to really feel with someone else.

Jesus wept.
JN 11:35

Crying is not a sign of weakness. Instead, a good healthy cry can be a sign of maturity. The real weakness is not allowing ourselves access to our emotions. Tears are miniature messengers (on call twenty-four hours a day) that fill those uncomfortable moments. They pour from the corner of our souls, carrying with them the deepest emotions that we possess. The principle is simple: When words are most difficult, tears are most appropriate.

Work for the Soul » Listen to the lyrics of the song "It's Okay to Cry" by Amanda Wilkinson. Print the lyrics and read them slowly. They are powerful.

Words from the Heart » *Dear God, I often cry with gratitude over the amazing gifts you've allowed to come my way. My tears have also helped me express my grief at the loss of those precious to me. Amen.*

March 27 | Monday, the Fifth Week
DANIEL 13:1–9, 15–17, 19–30, 33–62 • JOHN 8:1–11

Condemn No One

A married friend of mine was seen having a snack with a married man. Before she knew it, her coworkers were spreading false rumors that she was having an affair. This is an example of misunderstanding and poor judgment. Many of us have been guilty at one time or another of misjudging someone's behavior.

We see it in the story of the scribes and Pharisees who brought before Jesus a woman who was supposedly caught in the act of adultery. Witnesses were missing, yet many in the crowd (based on the accusations and hearsay of others) wanted to stone her to death.

> *"Woman, where are they? Has no one condemned you?"*
> JN 8:10

Like these people, we too are sometimes guilty of premature judgment when we spread a rumor that hasn't been verified, fail to correct faulty information, turn the spotlight on someone's failure, tell only one side of the story, or share only one dimension of a person's character.

When we don't always know all the issues, we need to resist the urge to judge or assume the worst. Accurate information is needed before we spread reports or twist someone's words. It means that we go to the person involved and get the facts before we draw the wrong conclusions.

We can stop making judgments and become more like Jesus. Rather than condemn this woman, he said to her accusers: "The one who is without sin among you should be the first to throw a stone." His words were so powerful. Not a single stone was thrown that day. Jesus has a clear message for all of us: it's about converting (not condemning), healing (not harassing), and forgiving (not fault-finding).

Work for the Soul » Every time you find yourself prematurely judging someone, stop and ask yourself, What would Jesus say?

Words from the Heart » *Dear God, I'm not going to judge others or expect them to be perfect, until I'm perfect myself. So, I guess everyone is safe, forever! Amen.*

March 28 | Tuesday, the Fifth Week
NUMBERS 21:4–9 • JOHN 8:21–30

You've Got a Friend!

In his book, Ed McMahon talks about Johnny Carson's loyalty to his friends. One friend, Burt Reynolds, was going through a difficult time in his life and most everyone had deserted him. But Johnny Carson remained constant, calling frequently to see how he was doing.

Often people say: "When I was going through this tough time, I learned who my real friends were." Friends are the people who are there for us when others are not. When the crowd dies down after a crisis, our friends are still there, active and involved. They stay with us through laughter, tears, good times, hardships, and difficult circumstances. Their loyalty holds and gets stronger with time.

> *"But he who sent me is reliable."*
> JN 8:26

Friends will motivate us! Margaret tells her friend, "Helen, you've been whining about the same thing for two months. It's time to get off your duff and do something about it." That's friendship!

Recently, I was sitting in my car in a parking lot (on a bright and beautiful day) and noticed a street lamp burning. They really need to turn that light off, I thought. Then it occurred to me: Friendship is a lot like that lamp. A real friend is someone who will shine for us all the time, regardless if we're in light or darkness.

Work for the Soul » Choose a day before Easter and make it "Friend Appreciation Day." Prepare a package that includes: a candle—to thank a friend for shining brightly when life was the darkest; a paper clip—in appreciation for helping you hold it together; and a Hershey's chocolate kiss—for all the love a friend has shared with us.

Words from the Heart » *Dear God, my friends are kind, honest, sensitive, loyal, understanding, caring, helpful, and always there for me. I want to be the same for them. Amen.*

March 29 | Wednesday, the Fifth Week
DANIEL 3:14–20, 91–92, 95 • JOHN 8:31–42

One Small Kindness at a Time!

A little starfish lay resting on the ocean floor talking to its mom and dad. "I was so scared," it said. "The current just grabbed me and threw me on dry land. I kept calling you over and over but you couldn't hear me. You won't believe what happened next. God picked me up and threw me back home!"

Just one person can make a *huge* difference in the lives of others! What does it take? Your decision to do so! Make the commitment to make a difference and take action!

Mary Ellen gives surprise gifts to her coworkers with notes telling them that they matter. She said: "It isn't much: a candy bar, cookie, or flower. I have fun letting them know that they're special."

We can offer acceptance, encouragement, or a simple smile. Just believing in others and supporting their goals and dreams is huge for them. A few kind words can soothe their pain. One caring person could literally save someone's life.

> *"If you hold to my teaching, you are really my disciples."*
> JN 8:31

We may never know how our actions (at just the right moment) can have a tremendous long-term impact. There are so many ways we can touch people's lives, with ideas, counsel, love, support, and belief that will help them along their journey. And, the interesting thing is that once we touch the life of just one person, they may go out and do the same.

Work for the Soul » You don't have to take on the whole world by yourself. Just do one small kindness at a time. Your action can have far-reaching consequences that you may never know about.

Words from the Heart » *Dear God, when I'm kind to someone, I hope they'll remember and be kind to someone else. And perhaps the ripple effect will spread. Amen.*

March 30 | Thursday, the Fifth Week
GENESIS 17:3–9 • JOHN 8:51–59

Just the Facts, Please

After his divorce, Ronnie said that he wanted to learn from his mistakes. He read books about divorce, attended recovery programs, and even spoke about his experience at singles' groups. But despite these efforts, he wasn't being completely honest with himself. He didn't want to face his role in the breakup. Instead, he blamed his ex-wife for every problem that occurred in the marriage. He refused to admit that his workaholic attitude played a significant role in unraveling the relationship.

When we allow ourselves to get caught up in hiding the facts, we no longer are able to make healthy choices. A nurturing, lasting relationship must be based on honesty. If not, it can be especially painful and difficult. At one time or another, many of us have been in relationships where conversations were labored, words were twisted, or emotions were exaggerated.

> *"I tell you the truth, if anyone keeps my word, they'll never see death."*
> JN 8:51

Avoid any misunderstanding. Any doubt created will inhibit the continued growth of love and trust. Being truthful can help us feel secure and bring us the necessary confidence needed for a long-lasting relationship. Only the truth (painful though it may be) can create a safe environment for unity and growth.

If we lie to the one we love, it may do more than just hurt. It may be totally devastating! We may be tempted to withhold the facts from time to time, but we should not. Use these temptations as learning experiences to practice more candid behavior. If we want our relationships to grow, genuineness must be our first goal.

Work for the Soul » For the next twenty-four hours, be totally and completely honest, no matter what. Tell the whole truth. Be gentle, yet direct and honest. Say what you mean, and mean what you say.

Words from the Heart » *Dear God, help me always tell the truth about myself and recognize it in others. Amen.*

March 31 | Friday, the Fifth Week
JEREMIAH 20:10–13 • JOHN 10:31–42

Be Who You Are

In his book *Wind, Sand and Stars*, Antoine de St. Exupéry has this wonderful quote: "Perhaps love is the process of my leading you gently back to yourself." This is truly what love is all about, being reminded of your true essence, uniqueness, and beauty.

On this journey back to yourself, avoid those who undermine you and attempt to leave you depressed and defeated. They will call you names, compare you to others, make you the focus of gossip, and stab you in the back. Avoid those who remind you of your past, who create shame and guilt by pushing your buttons. They will try to take you back to past scars, mistakes, blunders, missed opportunities, and bad decisions.

It's time to oust these people from your life and discover your God-given individuality and talent. Avoid the temptation to be what others want you to be. If you don't lead your own life, someone else will lead it for you. If you truly believe that you are not unique, others will take over, and then, you really will be lost. Just look these people in the eye and say: "Here I am! Accept me with all my faults. And if you can't do that, leave me alone."

> *"What about the one the Father set apart as his very own and sent into the world?"*
> JN 10:36

Work for the Soul » Sit down, close your eyes, and imagine yourself sitting next to you. Take three to four minutes to do this. What are you feeling? Notice how you felt when you looked at yourself. To counter any negative feelings, say: "I love myself. I accept myself unconditionally. I believe I'm God's child." Then be still, and wait for God to whisper, "I love you."

Words from the Heart » *Dear God, you proclaimed me at my birth as excellent. You know my name! I can now declare, "I am wonderfully made." Amen.*

April 1 | Saturday, the Fifth Week
EZEKIEL 37:21-28 • JOHN 11:45-56

Strolling Down Memory Lane

Many of us have unpleasant memories that will last forever—an accident, a horrible breakup, or the betrayal by a friend. Let the painful memories in. They are part of us and it's a permanent connection. I have a scar on my arm where I slammed through a window at the age of nine. It reminds me of the four hours the doctors needed to sew my arm back together. That scar is part of me. That experience is a permanent memory.

> *"They had seen what he had done and began to believe in him."*
> JN 11:45

The good news is that wonderful experiences and times of joy are also held in our memory banks—catching lightning bugs as a kid, that first kiss, or the time we held a newborn baby. Let those memories in also.

One of the best ways to create memories is to form family rituals. Perhaps a ritual can become part of your daily greeting or good-bye. Or, there could be a regular ritual performed at bedtime. It doesn't matter what you do, as long as you do it on a consistent basis so that it becomes a family tradition.

Brian has a ritual with his five-year-old daughter. He plays a giggly game and describes his love for her: "I love you as much as 10,000 walruses," he says. He hopes that in the future, when perhaps he can't tell her out loud how much he loves her, he can at least whisper: "One million elephants" and perhaps get a smile.

Create your own rituals. Celebrate birthdays, holidays and events that will bring your family together. These valued moments make memories positive and permanent.

Work for the Soul » Create special memories by spending time together as a family. Start your family rituals today that will always be remembered tomorrow.

Words from the Heart » *Dear God, my memories help me hold onto the things I love and the things I never want to lose. Amen.*

April 2 | Palm Sunday

MATTHEW 21:1–11 • ISAIAH 50:4–7 • PHILIPPIANS 2:6–11 • MATTHEW 26:14—27:66

Go with the Flow!

Life is so unpredictable. We can perceive it as limiting or something that unfolds with infinite possibilities. We can never be sure of what the next moment will bring. This uncertainty causes us to spend our lives worrying about possible outcomes, most of which are beyond our control.

Some of us overcome doubt by becoming perpetual planners. We relentlessly schedule for months and even years in advance. If we could be more willing to allow people, situations, and events to unfold naturally, they might bring an element of surprise into our highly structured lives.

> *"So you could not stay awake with me for even an hour?"*
> MT 26:40

Uncertainty causes us to seek outside ourselves for strength and control. We build impressive bank accounts, climb power ladders, and collect prestigious titles in an effort to overcome fear of the unknown and acquire some sense of security.

We secretly admire the powerful, emulate the successful, and seek out those who appear to be prosperous. If we had their money, fame, and strength, our fears would vanish. Then, we're devastated to learn that when we do have more wealth, fame, and power, nothing has changed.

Accepting life as it comes allows us to understand our frustrations and grow from them. We hear people say: "I go with the flow." What they mean is this: I accept in life what I cannot change. We must be willing to let go of the life that we've planned in order to make room for the one that is waiting for us.

Work for the Soul » Give yourself some slack time in your routine. If you plan everything down to the minute, things will be delayed when the unexpected happens. But if everything flows smoothly, you can use that slack time to be productive and creative.

Words from the Heart » *Dear God, help me not to cry because today is over. Instead, help me to smile because it happened. Amen.*

April 3 | Monday of Holy Week
ISAIAH 42:1–7 • JOHN 12:1–11

Unload Your Stuff

When my friend's home burned, he was allowed to go inside one last time to decide what to take with him. Years of stuff had accumulated, yet he only had enough time to gather some valuable papers, rush out the door, and never look back. A firefighter shared with me what people sometimes take as they frantically escape to safety: a television, grocery coupons, a toolbox, family albums, kitchen utensils, antique furniture, and personal letters. One man retrieved his daughter's favorite toy, a teddy bear she couldn't sleep without.

Too often we determine our worth by how many things we possess and their monetary value. We become so attached to our belongings that we sometimes allow them to control us.

We overflow with stuff in every part of our lives. So hungry are we for acquiring stuff, and so great is our attachment to it, that we are willing to rent space to hold it, sometimes miles away from our homes. In letting things go, we find excuses: I'm trying to figure out what to do with it. I might need it someday. I'm going to lose weight and wear it then.

"Mary took expensive perfume, she poured it on Jesus' feet and wiped his feet with her hair."
JN 12:3

We have four choices when it comes to letting go: trash it, give it away, sell it, or store it. The question to ask is this: Do I use it? The answer is simple: yes or no! The hard part about letting go is getting started, but once you do, magic will begin.

Work for the Soul » What would you salvage today if you only had a few moments to gather your things? You will learn a great deal about yourself doing this exercise.

Words from the Heart » *Dear God, sometimes my stuff holds me back from looking deeply into what is important in my life. I'm going to take stock, downsize, and simplify things. Amen.*

April 4 | Tuesday of Holy Week

ISAIAH 49:1-6 • JOHN 13:21-33, 36-38

The Deepest Hurt of All

The infidelity of a spouse, the harsh words of a parent, the failing of an aging body, or the devastation of a lost job—many of us have had these experiences of betrayal. They rock our world and bring forth feelings of resentment, bitterness, and emotional distance.

We can punish ourselves by focusing on the hurt and keeping it fresh with daily reminders. Or we can eventually let go and come to peace with the overwhelming emotion. Forgiveness is our best hope to return a relationship back to trust. It requires courage and a major shift in awareness. If we forgive, we can reclaim the peace of mind that comes from being free. We don't have to excuse the action that we experienced or deny the painful feelings. In fact, we must bravely and totally acknowledge the behavior in order to know when we're ready to let go.

"I tell you the truth, one of you is going to betray me."

JN 13:21

Forgiveness does not require that we allow the betrayer back into our lives. For a broken trust to heal, we must make a strong commitment to allow new behavior to happen. We must make it very clear what is acceptable in our life and what is not.

Forgiveness is a journey. Be patient and gentle with yourself. You may need some time before you are completely healed, but the nice thing is that you get better every day.

Work for the Soul » Resentment and bitterness are hard to let go of. Sometimes, a statement of intent is necessary: "In the name of God, I hereby forgive you for betraying me." Say this out loud, sincerely, several times a day.

Words from the Heart » *Dear God, help me to never forget that trust takes years to build, but only a second to break. Amen.*

April 5 | Wednesday of Holy Week

ISAIAH 50:4–9A • MATTHEW 26:14–25

Guess Who's Coming to Dinner?

When I asked a group of second- and third-graders: "What do you think makes a happy family?" They replied: "doing things together." Mealtime provides a great opportunity to interact with your kids and the people you love. The daily ritual of dining together and putting your knees under the same table is so important.

During family mealtime, you can share the best and worst parts of your day. You can plan a family activity or discuss options for your next vacation. Table time together provides everyone the opportunity to relax, belong, and be accountable to one another.

A woman told me: "Since my son is a single dad with two teenagers, we've been having Sunday dinner together for years. During that time, I've seen changes in my grandsons. They say 'please' and 'thank you' and clear the table without being asked. Sometimes they even help me fix dinner."

> "The Teacher says: 'My appointed time is near. I am going to celebrate the Passover with my disciples.'"
> MT 26:18

We've all heard the saying: Families that pray together stay together. It also turns out that families who dine together are emotionally and spiritually fine together.

So turn off that television. Power-down your laptop and forget about your voicemail messages. Just slow down, gather the family together at your table tonight, and bow your heads to thank God for the meal before you and the people beside you.

Work for the Soul » Create family placemats. For them, ask your children to draw a picture of the favorite part of their day. Older children may want to add puzzles or trivia they have learned. Adults may want to include birthdays or inspirational quotes or prayers. During dinner, allow everyone a chance to share his or her placemat.

Words from the Heart » *Dear God, dinners are more than just sharing food. They're times to help us get know each other. We will always cherish our family mealtimes together. Amen.*

April 6 | Holy Thursday
EXODUS 12:1–8, 11–14 • 1 CORINTHIANS 11:23–26 • JOHN 13:1–15

Be an Encourager

When Larry used to cry uncontrollably as a baby, his mother would burst into song with the words of the hymn, "Troublesome times are here." I think she was onto something. We face troublesome times. There are everyday troubles: being ill, not having enough money, being heckled at school, or feeling unappreciated.

Then there are more serious troubles: the tumor they found, your company downsizing, your marriage on the rocks, a single daughter expecting, or your parents moving in with you.

So many people feel discouraged, unworthy, unlovable, or completely overwhelmed when they encounter difficulties. We all face those moments, hours, or even days when our hearts take a nosedive and our world looks bleak.

In troubled times, be an encourager! Nothing can place a value on your uplifting words to a lonely person, a friend who's upset or afraid, or a relative or neighbor who is hospitalized or homebound.

Words of hope include: "You'll make it through," "I believe in you," "God is with you and will help you." As an encourager, share with others that hope in themselves, coupled with hope in God, is the anchor that holds them strong in the storms of life.

"I have set you an example that you should do as I have done for you."
JN 13:15

Work for the Soul » You have been blessed with at least one gift that you can share with others. If it's music, go to a day care or nursing home and entertain those with lonely, eager hearts. If it's physical strength, offer to help your elderly neighbor with her yard. If it's cooking, make a spaghetti dinner for someone who is going through a tough time. If you have money, give to someone you know in need, anonymously or with a card and a hug.

Words from the Heart » *Dear God, I want to encourage others and provide them with a shoulder to lean on. I want those who are struggling to feel special and cared for. Amen.*

April 7 | Good Friday

ISAIAH 52:13–53:12 • HEBREWS 4:14–16; 5:7–9 • JOHN 18:1–19:42

The Time to Live Is Now

Death. It's the one topic that many of us spend our lives avoiding. We're not comfortable discussing it. We never know how or when it will come. No matter how prepared we feel we may be, it always seems to take us by surprise. Yet, death is the greatest of life's teachers.

Death reminds us that nothing in this world belongs to us, especially other people. They will depart when it's their time no matter how loudly we protest. Too often, we blame them for leaving us and keep their memory alive through our feelings of remorse over what wasn't said. The most regretful phrase in our language is: "I should have." Yesterday is gone and yearning will never bring it back.

When someone is dying and surrounded by family, he or she will usually say things like, take care of your mother, check in on your brother, remember, I love you. Death is a reminder to express our love for each other while we still can. It arrives at our doorstep with a message: The time to live (and love) is now.

> *"Jesus said: 'It is finished.' Then he bowed his head and died."*
> JN 19:30

Death teaches us that the quality of time we spend together is so important. It will be hard to make up for lost moments, when they are gone forever. No matter what has happened in the past, we can begin again. Every day is new.

Work for the Soul » There's real value in discussing death as simply part of the cycle of life. Share your thoughts about death with family and close friends. Take your spouse and children to a cemetery, visit family graves, and share stories of relatives who have died.

Words from the Heart » *Dear God, my life is a gift from you. When you want it back, I have no right to complain. Amen.*

April 8 | Easter Vigil

GENESIS 1:1—2:2 • GENESIS 22:1–18 • EXODUS 14:15—15:1 • ISAIAH 54:5–14 • ISAIAH 55:1–11 • BARUCH 3:9–15, 32—4:4 • EZEKIEL 36:16–17A, 18–28 • ROMANS 6:3–11 • MATTHEW 28:1–10

Do Not Be Afraid

On that first Easter morning, everyone who heard the news was frightened—the guards, the religious leaders, and even Jesus' closest friends. Some ran directly to the source to verify that the news was accurate.

Others experienced fright, the kind of fear that totally incapacitates us. It can keep us from working, leaving our comfort zones, or being productive. That Easter Sunday, I'm sure many were in the fright mode. They were afraid to leave their homes and frightened out of their wits about what might happen next.

When we live a fright-filled life, it can stop us from experiencing new and exciting opportunities. It influences our choices by making us too cautious, conservative, and controlling. We're held captive within our own boundaries.

Don't allow fear to control you. It's okay to be scared out of your socks at times, yet you can still control your actions regardless of your feelings. It's not always easy, but it is a choice that you always have! Have faith. The ultimate fear-stopper is your belief that God is in charge of all things and is constantly at your side. Happy Easter!

> *"The angel said to the women, 'Do not be afraid, for I know that you are looking for Jesus, who was crucified. He is not here; he has risen.'"*
>
> MT 28:5–6

Work for the Soul » Take whatever steps you can to change the circumstances that cause your fear. If you're afraid of being alone, reach out to others and help meet some of their needs. When you sense your heart filling with fear, ask yourself: "What is causing this feeling?" Pinpoint the source and then try to deal with those issues.

Words from the Heart » *Dear God, may your words: "Do not be afraid" ring in my heart always. Amen.*

ALSO BY JOSEPH SICA

Fr. Joe Sica believes that no matter how deep our sorrows, how big our mistakes, or how firmly we hold on to our grudges, Jesus always stands ready to help us free ourselves so that we can live in love, forgiveness, and joy. Filled with humor, prayer, real-life stories, and very practical steps, *Your Guide to a Happy Life* brings together some of Fr. Joe's most powerful reflections to help you reach for the loving, joyous life Jesus wants you to have.

80 PAGES | $12.95 | 5½" x 8½" | 9781627855648

TO ORDER CALL 1-800-321-0411
OR VISIT WWW.TWENTYTHIRDPUBLICATIONS.COM

TWENTY-THIRD PUBLICATIONS
A division of Bayard, Inc.